VICTORY

VICTORY

Ben Kopel

H_NGM_N BKS
www.h-ngm-nbks.com

FIRST H_NGM_N EDITION, January 2012

ISBN 978-0-9832215-5-5

Book and cover design by Nate Pritts and Scott O'Connor
Artwork © Patrick J. Reed
Author photo © Mara Gold

TABLE OF CONTENTS

You can't win, you can't draw,
sometimes you can't even lose,
but to even train up to such a fight
is Victory.

Alan Dugan

I'll give you one tip: use your fists.

Patti Smith

GYMNASIUM OF THE SACRED HEART

Two boys, wearing track jackets,

with shaved heads and smooth hands,

are breathing Pine-Sol out of

a plastic bag and breaking

into a car with coat hangers.

Sad, thin-skinned kids with flammable

names and feathers for lungs.

Who tape their regrets to the top of the Atari.

Who write out their girlfriends' names in gasoline.

Who take a match to the front yard

before cutting a path through police tape

to get to a tall, cool, catholic school gym.

From the bleachers they stand as if to say

I sing for the canary gassed beyond belief

in the basement of the biology building.

I scream City of Love! City by the River!

Don't disown your skinny fisted sons

locked inside the locker room.

They too are the father of you.

They too are made mostly of noise.

The holiest of headaches has begun to flower

behind their eyes, and their fingers,

they are twitching like a clinic in the winter.

DUENDE-TRIPPER

Decapitate the headlights, I did

so our bodies could alone float free
away from the blacked-out city.

My darkness, it expanded

to fill the space provided, like a melody
or a metal rod placed in a loved one.

Some summer ago, the surgeons

they shoved a goodbye into my jaw.
There was confetti in the carpet.

A steak knife in the ceiling. So what.

So long. In between such stations
my life can save no song.

LIKE A SONG UNSUNG

without a sound I was born to make air bags bloom.
When I asked why
my mother told me I'll tell you when you're younger.
When I was younger
I found myself the only werewolf in a city made of
silver, spending Friday

afternoons keying my favorite name into car doors.
Do you have a name?
Do you have a head? My head is full of plastic fangs
and sheet music and
squirrel skulls. I hid the rest of their bones behind the
school because

I didn't want you to see me for what I was because I want
a clawfoot bathtub
full of what I want. You want to be incredible. If we are
to ever be together

you must walk out of this matinee with my head held

high above you while

there's still some daylight left outside of you.

CIAO MEIN, MORNING STAR

1.
Whiskey tango foxtrot,
pipsqueek yankee sweet-

heart! So strange it must be
to sing your own name. So

glad I am to have a pain
I can call all my own. A life.

My life. The life of it and the life
in it. No, not who am I but

what I was. One-third-dog.
One-third-man. One-third-

star. A mind out of time
and almost brave.

2.

Some bloom slum

later, high on Christ

and some kind of kindness

we two cross kites

and kiss against cars and

shine like a skulk of foxes

all warm skin warm

under a sky sans junk—

You: Roller-skate skinny

Me: A box of blood

DEAD BIRD TATTOO

What bird could be held

on the hand
in your arm

static, a suburb before—

& yet here I am
with you

not rotting.

THERE IS NO THERE THERE

I just work here.

Thick with hope

my mind is shut
and right and

always naming streets
after the people I love.

I hope. What is hope.

Hope is how I assassin

past drunken stadia
unshot by the sky.

Dumb from song.
Missing everybody.

START CUTTING BACK TODAY.
QUIT TOMORROW.

Before I exit the clinic

I pull the IV out of the dying boy's arm

& jam it into my own. An arm is an arm.

A day is a day, and gone is gone.

To die is no great indignity.

The world is flat if you want it to be.

I shot off my hand with my mouth

now I want to come home. So let me

come home. Kiss me in the parking lot.

I am full of love.

BECAUSE WE MUST

The kids from the federal
tanning booths have burned
down the Dairy Queen again.

Everyone died warm
& no one was alone.

::

We had a good time. I remember ice cream.
I remember legs. I remember gym shorts.

::

A prayer, now
& at the hour of our death—

Fill me with yr light inside this car.
Fill me with yr light.

FINAL BOY

Hollow-boned but

arms unbroken

I fly back to me

in v formation

my chest a flag

unfurled

and feathered

like the arrow

that longed to rest

its sharp skull

along the breast of

the final girl the

one my neighbor drowned

three separate times

in three separate rivers

in a body I could never

call my own

FINAL GIRL

I came back now I'm a goner
almost crucified successfully
inside unsatisfied suburba by
some unlovely fuck I was that girl
the one who said help me my boy
is missing I met him at the orientation
he met me at a bar called the foggy goggle
I called him birdbrain I called him sugar
skull and we were ugly and untrained
while he filmed me from the waist up his
whole system was nervous was a saint
operating on a surgeon with a box cutter
as sharp as a box cutter he told me
my new beauty was not only an early
riser but a bully as well as he pulled
a ski mask out of his back pocket
I told him charm me up to here hero

SWEETHEARTS

I bleached my hair in
the bathroom of a YWCA

and I was thinking about you
almost the entire time

beneath your swimsuit
there's an all-night diner

every waitress is a genius

::

outside your swimsuit
is the big country

seatbelts and student riots

sweetheart, gal Friday

the architect's beautiful daughter

I love you, but I hate your friends

VALENTINE

All expectations

drum roll

and meridians

I am

scared sacred

having nothing

to prove

to no

one waiting

for what

is not

gone to

go off

and on

until the

sun catches

me crying

the light

sees me

singing the

phonebook to

me myself

this freak

an accident

a heart

of hearts

UNTITLED

& what's the first
wish after every

t-shirt wrapped
around a fist

is plunged through
the passenger-side

window—
to not be loved

but to love
as one loves

to stay up late
smashing bottles

against the levee
for nothing

but feeling something

like the way

she must feel

as she

satellites around

the room

stabbing an avocado

with a spoon.

HIDDEN TRACK

to die
to know

you blinked
her eyelids

firm
precise

its joy

::

know me
never forget me

in spite of you
I salute you

your favorite tree

the wide garden

a breast

the ocean
a master

THE BIRTHDAY PARTY

At my favorite pharmacist's birthday party

there was this girl dressed up as a piece of wedding cake

that had been tucked in the freezer for a decade

who was telling me all about her family history.

She got to the part about the Holocaust but I thought

she said *hollyhocks* so I smiled while she switched

the subject to bodies of water and told me about

the time she got so high on scented markers

that she mistook a man-made lake for her mother.

I asked her about all the birthday candles in her hair

and she told me *one for every year he's in orbit* and

pointed to her fiancé, the astronaut puking over the

balcony. Later that evening, this new friend of mine

she followed me into the bathroom and tried to steal my

lighter. She said *In my dreams I'm always finding*

abandoned children in gas station parking lots

and state border rest stops and for this I loved her

but I had to be honest and pull away so that I could say

I'm still holding out for someone who knows where

I'm coming from what with all these ideas

I have about the conspiracy to keep me out of Space

Camp and this broken face I got from the worst

Field Day ever.

CVS SONNET

Gal Friday, aching to become, blankety-blank,
I mean this from the bottom of my blood.
Last night I hacked all the way to Madison
& you were always on my mind. In my dreams
there are seven hearts inside every boy. A metal
detector on Monday. A smoke detector by Friday.
Explosions on the flat screen in my time of need.

::

When will my store sell more than greeting cards
& muscle relaxers? I busted my hand
coming over the counter. Gal Friday, call the office.
Please tell them I'm broke. All of my friends'
fathers are dying. There's this hell inside my head.

::

How many bad incisions must be made
on my way to becoming a blade?

JOHN BERRYMAN DRUNK DIAL

No,

this is not that dream—

air slams air
& the author

he laughs &

me,

my smile gets smashed

::

No,

I'm not
falling

I'm not

nearly high enough

FRANK STANFORD SONNET

I dreamed I saw Frank Stanford
Last night & he said unto me

Shut up for a second so we can both
Be blinded by that bloody light

From the brainy motor
I call God's love.

::

He tossed a bottle over a bridge,
Pulled the hawk from under the hacksaw,

Reached the starling from the star
& pressed its beak into his palm.

He said. He said he got so alone sometimes
He believed God had a heart.

::

This morning

I found seven cicadas in my mailbox.

BAR FIGHT #2

Only because I felt like it—the
ashtray kid with seven hearts

cocked. Lit up and clockwork.
A face across my face.

My hands across your face.
Your ex-girlfriend

adjusting her wig at the bar.
Like clockwork. Part mutilation.

Part victory. Part garden.
Like the apology of a city

in your hands and
across my face.

THE DAY I WROTE YOU OFF

Today I take the bus
and buy nothing

from anyone behind
bulletproof glass.

I want to build
an altar out of small things.

I remove the stone
from my shoe

and place it in my mouth.
The sky is a skin.

I take the bus back
home. The rude boys

get busted and I think
my bad thoughts.

I slip my hand inside my shirt.
God is not an organ.

I take the stone from my mouth
and return it to my shoe.

I will always forget you.

AFTER PARTY

I came to
behind the
Five Happiness Buffet
with a black dog
stuck inside my ribs.

I pulled it out
by the roots
and started kicking
and kicking
and just kept on kicking
until the dog bloomed
hollyhocks.

I picked them
for my mom
and whispered
something
to myself

something

like happiness

happiness happiness

happiness happiness.

A MAP IS A PLACE IS A THING

We all recognize the need
to alter the ending.

We can and we will
even when we won't

let it become. We have no name.
Naming alone is understanding.

We have no idea. No book of legends.
No land. No map. We bracket sections,

combining longer and shorter lines.
We are left with what accounts for leaving.

We live the way we live.
The world changes us.

CONFESSIONAL POEM
FOR MARK LEIDNER TO READ

Sometimes in summer

a riot is born

& once again

we are skins versus skins.

Our truth is marching off

into the ocean

or a small room

with no windows.

I believe—

in every dream home

a blank stare.

A star is confused

for something still living

& I live to forget this.

These days I remember

you are so much like me.

I am quite nice.

Staircase wit.

Weak stomach.

Wires for temples

& photos with engines.

I have the best of intentions.

I believe in torture

& I will.

LIKE A JEW IN A TATTOO SHOP

I gawk.
You go

& on that note
you left a bag
of swimsuits

in the back of my car.

I can drive all night
but can't tie a tie
to save my life.

Tube-fed.
Gun-shy.

Next thing
I know I
pull over to the shoulder.

I toss my revolver

& my ring

into the river.

I don't go swimming.

I gawk.

POP SONG AUGHT SEVEN

Give me some

white teeth

& a black flag

to match

these red eyes

& simple, blue heart

& I don't mean

to fuck anyone

over

but

I can't be clever

all the time

TURN OFF MY FACE

hardcore clusterfuck mister
funny ha ha wanna gimme
gimme gimme scratch that
acne sucking down soba
noodles at the all ages show

widdle man him wanna kizza
on miz scooter on gal's soft little
target y'know like BANG
ZAP BANG hardcore
clusterfuck mister funny
ha ha gonna gimme gimme

gimme lick my battery mutha
gotta face so cute he gonna slice
all y'all up in yr cars
all y'all shitheel sons inna circle
pit gotta give some wuv

for widdle ol hims in hi-

fidelity hardcore cluster-

fuck mister funny ha ha wanna

gimme gimme gimme back my baby

see she sucking down on soba

noodles at the all ages show

ACADEMY FIGHT SONNET

You can eat skin.

You can drink water from a jug.

You can learn how to drive a truck.

You can call me a fascist

but one day we will stop hating ourselves

so much. We will forget the fight song & admit

the year of the waitress was a great one.

::

I was the change boy at your laundromat.

I wanted control of my body so

I did a thousand sit-ups. Then I died.

It's all right. I'm not even there.

Does the body rule the mind or

does the mind rule the body?

I don't care.

DO YOU WANT NEW SINCERITY
OR DO YOU WANT THE TRUTH?

Fuck, man

here I stand

punchdrunk

squibbed

trepanned

7 hearts

7 kinds

of a bastard

the worst

17 year old

in the whole

wide world—

the china

shop inside

the bull

the bird

house inside

the bird

& still alone

alone & still

singing.

THE DAY THE AMBULANCE CAME

He is on his last dime while the agents monitor
the signal and sketch his origin into receipts,
parked near parts of himself cradled in vaseline
next to the microphone they installed in the bathroom
floor.

Downtown, a payphone has been ringing since the day
the bombs dropped. He can walk miles to the receiver
and never leave the bed. The bed is his brain.
The mattress is strapped

to his skull. Stuck for days. No way
to hold hand to head so he can speak
to the question mark on the other end of the line,
to tell them about his plan to care for the world,

and the smell of oxygen fresh from the tank
and how it tastes to turn the pages
of a boring book with your tongue.

He falls asleep reading a manual

for out-of-date software while laughing boys

burn their leaves in the bathtub. Sophomore

skinned daughters of the cul-de-sac trot

the pavement, pitiless of the architect of those ugly

new houses, watching from a window, his pervert suit

shining like a motorcade of headlights.

THE CRICKETS

The detectives are awkward.
They should be.

Crickets are awkward.
Tanning bed step-mothers

crisping in those violent
bulbs are awkward— you are as well.

Random love shifts awkwardness
by the beams of aforementioned

awkwardness:
One folds one's shirts

on the bed of their awkwardness
and lets the detectives know. The crickets

strum their permanent tunes.

You engage your knowledge of sound

for an agency and this is

so much more; you will let the detectives know.

You save your love of true insects

for awkward silences.

RATIO

Your body
was bright

with one last
signal-to-noise

from the tape
head heart

as its beating
grew weaker

than the speakers
of this student

loan stereo
the drum machines

never sounded
sweeter than they did

coming out
from over the radio

the one place
where I was

always at my
most handsome

BLUE HEART PLASTIC

1.

Industry professionals can make any room
look like a waiting room. If the set wasn't so full,
I could make the viewers at home believe

I'm comfortable in another man's uniform—
an asthmatic firefighter, a glorified walk-on.

The way extras mingle makes me think
of the plastic Oscar on my mantle
awarded to The World's Best Secretary by

a saint who understood my unironic love
for another c-list actress, Burn Victim #4,
her tongue a sad finger tracing bad dialogue.

2.

If I had my way all thumbs present
and accounted for would oppose

to give idle threats equal billing
on hairline triggers. This is the method.
This is the problem. This is the firefighter

four hours in the chair. Five beers deep.
Clutching his inhaler. Waiting for his makeup
to set before he walks to the set.

3.

Was I born in a room just like this one where

real spines glisten when called to raise arms as

Burn Victim #4 walks into the office with her

eyes spread to a fireman's blue heart shining

in plastic wrap. This place has so many habits

that crack an actor, hip bones pressed against the

arcade machine, guts stuffed with quarters for days.

Out there is always moving. My lungs are sticking

and my coworkers videotape every second of it.

4.

Burn Victim #4 and I fight like kid sisters

and drop the script before I even have a chance

to show her the house I grew up in. We are both in love,

just not with each other. I've lost my inhaler

but I found her sterilized hands holding my face

to the floor. I'm not young but I am fine and I can

twist my spine just so, so I can see a studio audience

member fall silent and at once become

the most beautiful thing in all of Los Angeles

for the first time in his entire life.

THE HAPPIEST DAYS OF MY LIFE

The happiest days of my life

were those when ugliness

found no lit vacancy,

and I spent the night fukt

inside your skinny arms.

THE STREET SONNET

Oh my God my friends. Oh my God the world
my friends the world is a sad place to be tonight.
The world is this way but what if the world
was a girl? The world could be a girl who is sad
and lovely and in love with some strange boy.
And if this world were a vein the boy and the girl
would belong inside this vein that is the world.
Inside the vein there would be blood and the boy
and the girl and they could be alone inside of the world.

::

My friends
the world isn't a girl. The world isn't a girl
in the street at night. The world won't be a girl
in the street at night until my heart becomes
the street. My heart becomes the street at night.

TEENAGE VICTORY POEM

Way down deep inside the bored demographic,

a girl who's all Halloween and hardware

and a handsome young skater make tracks

all the way to a Motel 6 with hours to burn

to fill up a bucket with some dirty cubes

of ice that they can call the bad memories

of his summer-sore wrist. She ripped her lucky

tour t-shirt when they went swimming, the two

of them all clavicle and nipple from the waist

straight up, the six-pack rings wrapped around

their wrists shocking the sleeping salesmen,

spilling their paperwork across their pornography

while her father woke up across the city

just in time to greet the garbage men.

And as the lonesome sun rose over the local

nuclear reactor, the two of them made some great

noises together while two pairs of jet black jeans

dried out along a banister.

THERE IS A QUESTION I AM FOREVER
WAITING TO BE ASKED

& the only answer

goes something like this—

In the attic of everything

there is a bird

with one wing

& his heart is true

& nothing like mine.

DEEP CUT

In slow motion
and far from me
a porn star eats
a piece of candy.

May my greatest hits
be written in vaseline.
May every post-teen pump
his or her way towards a life.

When my enemies
decode this
it should only say
good boy.

POEM STRAPPED TO THE RADIATOR
FOR MAKING TOO MUCH RACKET

Fat boy broke

his leg chasing

the ice cream truck.

I slapped him hard

on the sunburn

across his back.

It felt good

seeing him so slow.

Being his brother.

Only children

hurting housecats

in the summertime.

WHY I AM NOT A TIGER

You are not a truck stop.

We have a wedding to get to
so meet me in the gift shop
& bring what you have inside you.

I have twenty-two muscles in my smile.
I am never lonely. There is no light
machinery inside of me. No hive
& no honey.

No academy. Nothing like the tiger we found
in the center of the city.

WHY I AM NOT A TIGER [version]

I built a toy coffin

for the poor killed kitten

out of the fifty-four bones I found

inside your hands.

What I bury

stays buried.

What I see

I've seen.

I have been the child-

bride stripped bare (again

& again) & if I could see myself at thirty

I would tell him

I will be good soon. Alright?

Alright.

ONE POEM THREE TIMES

1.

Somewhere near the scattering area

and gashed apart by beauty

my friends will always worry about me.

We surround each other like air, like I don't know.

2.

I hate this town. The orchestra

is empty. The geeks know nothing.

From heated pool to open bar in

true waltz time I want to walk away.

3.

Gasoline hearted, spark thrown.

People have no faith in people.

This is my mistake, my request:

Let me hang you from my rearview.

ELEGY FOR LESTER BANGS

As soon as

the punks

have attained

no future

the beach

it will

break free

up from under

the concrete

the high beams

inside the stag

will shine

on and on

and when all

is said and

all is done

I would rather die

at the movies

than in one

INVINCIBLE COYOTE

The cartoon hopeful

allowed the animators

to run him through

with a hollow pipe

in the middle of his audition.

He got some good laughs

and a solid score, but failed

to make callbacks.

He thanked the crew

and left the studio

to catch the five-fifteen.

He was miserable in his seat,

having forgotten to ask someone

to be so kind as to remove

the pipe before he boarded.

A radioactive boy who grew up

near the local nuclear reactor

stepped into his shadow and offered

to remove the offending

length from the coyote's belly.

A crowd gathered around them.

This time he was not brave.

The pipe was in his center,

maybe holding important things

in their painted places.

But he was a good cartoon.

The glowing boy knew it to be true

as only the good cartoons

are given shadows.

It's like swords and stones, the pipe

sliding out and the coyote sighing

and the crowd cheering

and the boy whispering

You are something so beautiful.

You belong in one of those

Technicolor landscapes

my ancestors dreamed up.

FOR ROBBIE

Every time

he starts the car

the click and ah

of the air conditioner

gives him hope

for a better tomorrow

in America—

the possibility

of a Dixie cup

filled with water

from a Japanese glacier

NO SURRENDER SONNET

& it's not because my father sells knives
that no one can ever become what they never

were. Like some unlovely kid who kills the party
& comes stumbling home resplendent, I too

wake up with my best friend's blood staining
my shoes. There are pieces of someone all over

the highway & still Frankie Lymon sings
about something called love. All the whores

are still warm, still full of shotgun songs.
Always missing. Never lost. Reaching back

into the back seat to hit me hard &
to see my face & to know my number

so we can call this place by its one true
name—shanty-town, shanty-town, shanty-town

CLAYTON ALLYNN

To bless his brain
to stop that mind

from taking the time
to dip the car in kudzu.

There isn't any windshield
just screened in stars.
Farm winds blanket churches

& it kills me—
how kids can be so cruel.

The director doesn't want to know
himself any better

but from what stone the producers
found inside his head

he has fashioned us a prairie

populated with wild dogs
& missing children.

SUBURBAN FIELD RECORDINGS

St. Julee reached for the radio while Zack the Lion
sketched a swastika on the back of a leaf. With some
stick pins and cinnamon flavored floss they took turns
stitching it to the passenger seat. They left the toys in the
yard and ran screaming through the parish, covering
their heads with a cardboard cut-out of Field
Commander Kopel, the one whose idiot kiss they could
both barely remember. Out past the party lights they
came across a chord organ hidden in the cane and
started composing a song for the Field Commander to
sing while he sets his face on fire somewhere in Johnson
County. St. Julee sang *Tonight I want / to see all my
friends / Love never begins / It doesn't even go / Say
goodbye / Hello* while Zack the Lion pointed his favorite
finger back to the yard, back to the car, back to the leaf
that was supposed to be the Field Commander's
heart and he swore to St. Julee on his stepbrother's
biography to fail each day closer to the bone than he
began, with a flare gun shoved in his sock and his hand
stuck in the till.

SONG OF JOY SONNET

Divided by the light pouring out of another sick
son-of-a-salesman tied to a tree a few feet away
from me—I stand disco-napped, tagged and bagged.
The rose garden in my side is good and gone,
bought and sold by the bullet that bit the gun.

::

With one hand nailed to the wind, I now know
no back should be born with a spine so soft.
A pair of lungs some daughter's father fixed up.
A line in his left arm leading straight to twenty-
eight chambers pumping seven quarts of blood.

::

From the target of my t-shirt I tell my ill friend
you will wake up. You will wake up and
you will run. You will run and you will rise.
Like the sun. Like a star. A nova. An idiot.

AMEN.

When I die
I will die

Escaping
Nearly blooming

Under a methane
Fed sunset

Cinematic

Straight past
The slaughterhouse

A pillowcase
Full of coyote skulls

Tied loose
Round my neck

CREDITS

Poems from *VICTORY* have previously appeared, in some form or another, in the following journals:

Diagram
Forklift: Ohio
Juked
The Agriculture Reader
Notnostrums
Thieves Jargon
H_NGM_N
Sixth Finch
Weird Deer
Invisible Ear
Make Out Creek
The New Delta Review
Conduit
La Petite Zine

Selections from *VICTORY* previously appeared in a chapbook titled *Because We Must,* which was part of the Coinside Library from Brave Men Press.

::

Also, psychic hearts go out to Dean Young, for gifting this book with its title.

ACKNOWLEDGMENTS

VICTORY would not have been possible without the faith and patience and generosity provided by all of my favorite past life martyred saints, including, but not limited to:

Mom and Dad and Josh, Adam Fell, Alex Chilton (1950-2010), Andrea Fortunato, Ann Marie O'Neill, Anne Cecelia Holmes, Betsy Shepherd, Brenda Hillman, Brett Eugene Ralph, Brett Jones, Brian Domingue and the rest of the River City Punks, Brian Foley, Bruce Springsteen, CA Conrad, Caroline Cabrera, Christen Mills, Christy Crutchfield, Christopher Ray, Clay Achee, Craig Finn, Dara Wier, David Berman, Dean Young, Del Dejean, Dobby Gibson, Dottie Lasky, Eef Barzelay, Emily Perkins, Emily Pettit, Ethan Guagliardo, Federico del Sagrado Corazón de Jesús García Lorca, Gabe and Liz Durham, Gabriel Rodriguez, Gale Thompson, Gertrude Stein, Gordon Massman, Graham Foust, Grant Morrison, Guillaume Apollinaire, Guy Pettit, Hugh O'Connor, Ian Curtis, Ian Reed, J.D. Salinger, Jack Christian, Jade Blank, James Haug, James Tate, James Weber, JAPANDROIDS, Jason Dupuy, Jeff Tweedy, Jenny Moore, Jimmy Driscoll, St. Joe Strummer, John Craun, John Darnielle, John Wygle, Joni Mitchell, Jordan Stempleman, Julee LaPorte, Katherine Treppendahl, Katie Perry, Kirstin Martinez, Laura Mullen, Lee Posna, Leonard Cohen, Lorraine Lorio, Luke Bloomfield, Mark Leidner, Mark Martin, Marty Sartini Garner, Matt Berninger, Matt Hart, Matt Heroman, Matthea Harvey, Matthew Suss, Meredith Harper, Michael Glaviano, Michael Russo, Michelle Taransky, Mike Roth, Mike Wall, Mike Watt and D. Boon, Nate Pritts, Patrick Jimmy Reed, Patti Smith, Paul

Knox, Paul Westerberg, Peter Gizzi, Randolph Thomas, Rebecca McCray, Robert Hass, Robbie Howton, Sampson Starkweather, Sarah Cancienne, Sarah Purnell, Scott O'Connor, Seth Landman, Steve Albini, Steven Patrick Morrissey, Susanna McBride, Terry Gilliam, Travis Morrison, Will Brideau, Will Scheff, Xtian Reader and Zack Arrington.

Thank you, friends.
Wouldn't be here if it wasn't for you.

Ben Kopel was born in Baton Rouge, Louisiana in 1983. He holds degrees from Louisiana State University, The Iowa Writers' Workshop, and The University of Massachusetts Amherst MFA Program for Poets and Writers.

He currently lives in New Orleans, Louisiana, where he teaches creative writing and English literature to high school students.

Made in the USA
Charleston, SC
10 March 2012